MAY -- 2016

D1032618

JOSEPH **STALIN**

Dictator of the Soviet Union

JOSEPH **STALIN**

Dictator of the Soviet Union

BY LINDA CERNAK

CONTENT CONSULTANT
STEVEN A. BARNES
ASSOCIATE PROFESSOR OF HISTORY
GEORGE MASON UNIVERSITY

Essential Library
An Imprint of Abdo Publishing | abdopublishing.com

abdopublishing.com

Published by Abdo Publishing, a division of ABDO, PO Box 398166, Minneapolis, Minnesota 55439. Copyright © 2016 by Abdo Consulting Group, Inc. International copyrights reserved in all countries. No part of this book may be reproduced in any form without written permission from the publisher. Essential Library™ is a trademark and logo of Abdo Publishing.

Printed in the United States of America, North Mankato, Minnesota

052015
092015

Cover Photo: AP Images
Interior Photos: AP Images, 2, 6, 10, 12, 18, 20, 24, 28, 30, 32, 42, 45, 48, 54, 63, 69, 70, 74, 82, 87, 92; Margaret Bourke-White/Time & Life Pictures/Getty Images, 14; North Wind Picture Archives, 17; Bettmann/Corbis, 36, 40, 57, 58, 64, 66, 84; Daily Express/Hulton Archive/Getty Images, 50; AFP/Getty Images, 60; B. Kudoyarov/Hulton Archive, 78; Keystone-France/Gamma-Keystone/Getty Images, 89; Mikhail Metzel/AP Images, 94

Editor: Arnold Ringstad
Series Designer: Becky Daum

Library of Congress Control Number: 2015934092

Cataloging-in-Publication Data

Cernak, Linda.
 Joseph Stalin: Dictator of the Soviet Union / Linda Cernak.
  p. cm. -- (Essential lives)
Includes bibliographical references and index.
ISBN 978-1-62403-896-9
1. Stalin, Joseph, 1879-1953--Juvenile literature. 2. Heads of state--Soviet Union--Biography--Juvenile literature. 3. Soviet Union--History--1925-1953--Juvenile literature. I. Title.
947.084/2/092--dc23
[B]   2015934092

CONTENTS

CHAPTER
ONE

THE RISE OF JOSEPH STALIN

Wintertime in Siberia is unlike that in most places on Earth. The bitter cold is bone-chilling—a few hours in it can bring certain death to those who are not adequately dressed. In the 1930s, horrific labor camps were established in this frozen land in the Russian north. They were filled with thousands of thieves, petty criminals, and murderers. But among the prisoners were also merchants, farmers, and people who simply disagreed with the government. A government agency known as the Gulag—a name that eventually became synonymous with the camps themselves—ran these labor camps. Prisoners were sentenced to hard and often deadly labor in unbelievably harsh conditions.

The freight trains arriving in the camps were packed with prisoners who had been carried hundreds or even thousands of miles away from their homes. They were forced to toil in mines, chop wood, and build canals.

By the end of the 1930s, there were dozens of Gulag labor camps in the Soviet Union.

Prisoners ate meager rations of bread and thin soup. Those who did not work hard enough received even less to eat. Many of those who managed to survive the ghastly working conditions still starved to death. In the span of a few decades, it is believed approximately 18 million people passed through the camps.[1]

Joseph Stalin was the man chiefly responsible for the Gulag camps. He led the Soviet Union for more than three decades. His oversight of the camps, along with his conduct during World War II (1939–1945), suggested he believed human lives were expendable. Stalin went down in history as a cruel, merciless tyrant. At the same time, he was remembered for modernizing a struggling country.

An Exchange of Power

On a cold winter day in 1924, Vladimir Lenin lay dying near Moscow. In the preceding decade he had led Russia through a Communist revolution, establishing the Soviet Union in 1922. But now three strokes had left him paralyzed and mute. On January 21, he finally died. The people of Russia mourned the death of their beloved leader. At the same time, Stalin, one of Lenin's longtime allies, began setting into motion the events that would lead to his seizure of power.

In 1924, a group known as the Central Committee ruled the Soviet Union. The Central Committee had the power to impact the daily lives of Soviet citizens. It exerted its power over the military, the police, factories, universities, shops, and businesses. Members of local Communist groups reported to the Central Committee and obeyed its commands. Local leaders were

THE END OF THE GULAG

Political prisoners remained in Soviet labor camps under harsh conditions well into the 1950s, though their numbers dropped sharply after Stalin's death in 1953. It was not until 1987 that General Secretary Mikhail Gorbachev ordered the last camp for political prisoners closed for good. Penal camps, holding largely ordinary criminals, continue to exist today.

Lenin, *left*, with Stalin a few years before Lenin's death

in charge of rewards and punishments, as well as jobs and apartment assignments. Whoever controlled the Central Committee effectively controlled the entire nation. Since the Soviet Union's establishment, Lenin had been in this position of control.

Stalin had been appointed general secretary of the Central Committee in 1922. At the time, it was not considered an important leadership position. Earlier general secretaries had performed standard secretarial or administrative work. Stalin spent his time in the office carefully positioning his supporters. He handed out jobs and favors to those he felt would side with him. He formed a network of spies that kept him informed about the activities of the Communist Party's leaders. The actions he took during this time would pay off after Lenin's death.

Fearing a split in the party, Lenin wrote a careful set of instructions regarding the party's future leadership. He planned to criticize Stalin and other party members at an upcoming party meeting. But his death prevented him from doing so in person. Instead, Lenin's words were read at a party meeting after his death. In the instructions, known as Lenin's Testament, Lenin

"LETTER TO CONGRESS"

Lenin wrote his "Letter to Congress" shortly before his death. As party leader, he wanted to make sure there would not be a split among the new rulers of the Soviet Union. In his letter, he discussed the qualifications of the party members who were most likely to take his place. Lenin had reservations about the leadership qualities of Stalin and wanted Stalin removed from his role as general secretary. His letter became known as Lenin's Testament. Lenin wrote the following about Stalin:

> Comrade Stalin, having become secretary-general, has boundless power . . . in his hands, and I am not quite sure whether he will always be capable of using that power with . . . caution.

> Stalin is too rude and this defect . . . becomes intolerable in a general secretary. That is why I suggest that the comrades think about a way of removing Stalin from that post and appointing another man in his stead who . . . differs from comrade Stalin . . . namely that of being more tolerant, more loyal, more polite, and more considerate to the comrades.[2]

Stalin, *left*, was solidly in control of the Soviet Union by 1930.

suggested Stalin be removed as general secretary. Since the position of general secretary was relatively unimportant at the time, Lenin likely did not expect Stalin to seek leadership. Still, Lenin's words could have meant the end of Stalin's career. In the end, however, party members kept Stalin in place. They sought not only to preserve party unity but also to divert attention away from Lenin's criticisms of themselves. It was a mistake they would soon regret.

A Dictator Rises

Upon Lenin's death, Stalin began to maneuver his opponents out of power. He allied himself with supporters to seize power and then had those who would rival him removed. Years later, he would resort to assassination and execution to rid himself of other leading party members. One of his chief rivals, Leon Trotsky, was killed in 1940 in Mexico by an assassin wielding an ice pick.

Through his maneuvering, Stalin became the leader of the Soviet Union. He would later be responsible for the deaths of millions in the labor camps of Siberia. Millions more would die on the battlefields of World War II, killed by the Nazis in such huge numbers in part because of Stalin's disregard for human life. His economic policies would cause one of the deadliest famines in history. He would also orchestrate the rise of a nation out of primitive poverty and into the ranks of modern industrial superpowers.

LENIN'S TOMB

Upon Lenin's death, the members of the Politburo—the top leaders of the Central Committee—had his body embalmed. The body was placed in a glass tomb for public viewing in a mausoleum in central Moscow. For decades, military parades marched past the building in celebration of the Communist leader. Today, visitors can still see the body of Lenin. There is some debate, however, as to whether it is the actual body or a wax replacement.

CHAPTER
TWO

A REVOLUTIONARY IN THE MAKING

At the center of the now-independent country of Georgia—once a part of Russia and subsequently the Soviet Union—is the city of Gori. Joseph Djugashvili was born into a peasant family in the town on December 6, 1878. His mother, Ekaterina, had lost her first two children, and she prayed fervently for her new son's survival. His father, Vissarion, was not a kind man. Vissarion beat Joseph and his mother often. Childhood for Joseph was harsh in other ways, too. The family was poor, living in a ramshackle hut on a dirt road. Like other peasants in Gori, they struggled to survive. Disease and death lurked in every corner of the town, and hunger was common. Gori was typical of thousands of other villages scattered across the vast expanse of Russia.

At that time, Russia was ruled by czars, a line of emperors who had controlled the nation for centuries.

Stalin's boyhood home in Gori was later encased in a marble shrine.

During their rule, the vast majority of Russians were peasants and serfs. The nobility had complete control over most of the land. They treated the serfs who farmed the land like slaves. By Joseph's time, the feudal system of serfdom had technically been abolished. But peasants of the 1800s were not much better off than the serfs of the Middle Ages. Peasants had few rights, if any, and feuds between them were often settled by swords and not by law. Even in cities, where factories and heavy industry were just beginning to grow, people lived in slums and worked under dreadful conditions.

Joseph's childhood was filled with other difficulties besides poverty. At the age of seven, he contracted smallpox, a terrible disease that left his face scarred. The beatings from his father caused him to suffer other physical injuries. It is believed Joseph's mother also beat him, even though she loved him dearly. The deep emotional scars from the beatings would last a lifetime.

Russian peasants lived primitive existences in the late 1800s.

Joseph's hatred of his father grew. He became involved with street gangs and bullied his schoolmates.

A Hotbed for Revolutionaries

Despite his difficult childhood, Joseph was an excellent student, and his mother had high hopes for his future. Her dream was for Joseph to enter seminary and become a priest. She believed it was the only way for her son to escape the dreary existence of peasant life. Joseph's hard work in school paid off. He was accepted at the seminary in the town of Tiflis, the capital of his province. Joseph entered the seminary in 1894 at the age of 16. But

Stalin's interest in politics began when he was a young man.

seminary life was not easy. The priests imposed severe rules on the students, sometimes even locking them up in solitary confinement as punishment. Young Joseph hated the seminary. But soon he would be exposed to ideas that would lead him to change the course of Russian history.

At the time Joseph was in seminary, there was a growing discontent among the peasants and workers of Russia. People were not happy living under the absolute power of the czar. The czar made the laws, appointed government officials, and had unlimited authority. There were no elections and no representation for the people of Russia. As industrialization began to spread into Russian cities, workers were subjected to appalling conditions in factories. Joseph became interested in these issues, and he associated with classmates who felt the same way.

CZAR NICHOLAS II

During Joseph's youth, Czar Nicholas II ruled Russia. Nicholas II was the last czar. The czars of Russia were members of a long line of rulers that began with Ivan the Terrible in 1547. Nicholas rose to the throne upon the death of his father in 1894. However, Nicholas was a weak ruler. Both his wife, Alexandra, and the mystic adviser Grigori Rasputin influenced his policies and manipulated his decisions.

The writings of Karl Marx would change the course of not just Stalin's life, but also the lives of millions of people around the world.

The Politics of Karl Marx

Joseph became interested in revolutionary thinking. He began reading works by leading thinkers and theorists. The writing of German author Karl Marx was especially fascinating to him. Marx's book *Das Kapital* was particularly explosive. In it he analyzed and criticized capitalism, explaining how he believed it would lead to socialism, a political and economic system in which the people control the means of production and distribution. This system was explained in *The Communist Manifesto*, written by Marx and Friedrich Engels. The Marxist theory stated that capitalists—the people who owned businesses, industries, and land—got rich by exploiting workers' labor. Marx felt the capitalists enslaved the

KARL MARX

Born in 1818, Karl Marx became involved with radical groups while living in Germany as a young man. His views were discussed in *The Communist Manifesto*, published in 1848. The work became a handbook for revolutionary groups throughout Europe. Soon after the publication of the book, Marx was forced to leave Germany. His views made him unwelcome in most European countries, so he sought refuge in London, England, in 1849. He would spend the rest of his life there. His work *Das Kapital* was published in 1867. Marx died in 1883.

Together, *The Communist Manifesto* and *Das Kapital* expressed Marx's political theories. He believed great changes in society were a result of changes in the economic system. He also believed society was a result of struggles between capitalists and the working class. As he explains in *The Communist Manifesto*: "The history of all hitherto [up until now] existing society is the history of class struggles."[1] Marx believed revolutionaries would have to take control of a government by force, because capitalists would not accept socialism peacefully. Eventually, after the Communist society was fully established, the government structure would simply vanish on its own.

workers. In time, according to Marx, the workers would revolt and destroy the capitalists. The workers would then own all businesses, industries, and land. There would be no profit, just people working for a common goal. Eventually a classless society would emerge. Everyone would contribute to the community according to his or her ability, and everyone would receive from the community according to his or her need.

No one would own private property. This system was known as communism. Marx believed the evolution into such a classless society was inevitable.

The ideas in Marx's revolutionary books and others began to shape Joseph's own thinking. However, the works were banned in the seminary. Joseph was caught reading forbidden books and was expelled from the seminary in 1899. But he had few regrets. He would never become a priest, and the rough life of a revolutionary suited him. Joseph aligned himself with fellow revolutionaries and supported workers' struggles. He enjoyed the protests, strikes, riots, secret meetings, and plots against the government. These activities eventually led to Joseph's arrest by the Okhrana, the czar's secret police. He was imprisoned in 1902 and would spend the next decade in and out of prison. It was during this time that he became influenced by another great revolutionary: Lenin. In his old age, Stalin declared, "If there'd been no Lenin, I'd have stayed a choirboy and a seminarian."[3]

CHAPTER
THREE

THE BOLSHEVIK REVOLUTION

During his years in and out of Siberian prisons, Joseph often traveled in disguise. He also used a variety of nicknames. One name, Koba, was based on a legendary Georgian bandit akin to Robin Hood. The name was appropriate because Joseph was often involved in bank and train robberies. These acts of violence and thievery were typical of the revolutionary tactics of the Russian Social Democratic Labor Party, whose purpose was to fight against the czar. Joseph joined the party in 1903. One of its leaders, Lenin, would eventually split from the main party to form the Bolshevik Party, a new faction. In 1905, Lenin had been a major figure in a failed Russian revolution. His wing of the party would later lead a successful revolution against the Russian government and become the Communist Party of the Soviet Union.

Stalin, *top row, middle,* began his revolutionary career as a minor member of a group of political exiles.

It was during a trip to Finland in 1905, where Joseph traveled in one of his many disguises, that he first met Lenin. Lenin was impressed with Joseph's brutal but effective methods and needed him to help raise money to support the Bolshevik cause. Funds paid for their campaigns against the czar, including the printing of underground newspapers, the bribery of some officials, and the assassinations of others. The work suited Joseph—he excelled as a gangster. Under his command, bombs were set off and banks robbed, all with the purpose of overthrowing the czarist regime that controlled the country. He also wrote and edited

VLADIMIR LENIN

Vladimir Lenin's childhood was much different from Stalin's. Lenin was born on April 22, 1870, into a well-educated upper-class family. He studied law at a university, but he was expelled from school for his revolutionary political views. Like Stalin, Lenin was an avid reader of Marx. However, Lenin's beliefs differed slightly from those of Karl Marx. While Marx felt revolution would take place when workers rose up against capitalists, Lenin believed there were not enough workers in Russia to successfully execute the revolution. Instead, he believed a small group of professional revolutionaries should control a central committee that would control the government of Russia. Lenin thought the central committee should also have a supreme commander—Lenin himself. He believed violence was necessary for revolution to take place. That was where Stalin fit in. Stalin was as ruthless as Lenin, and his talent for brutal violence served to keep the leadership of the revolutionary party in power.

newspaper articles in support of the revolution. During this time, Joseph took on another nickname. On a March 1913 article, he signed his name Stalin, which came from the Russian word for "man of steel." The nickname would follow him into history.

In the 1910s, there was a growing unrest among the people of Russia. Riots and strikes were common as a result of deplorable working conditions. There was a shortage of food, and the government was in a state of disorder. In 1914, Russia became involved in World War I (1914–1918). It entered the war on the side of the Entente powers, which included the United Kingdom, France, and eventually the United States. These nations fought the Central powers, including Germany, Austria-Hungary, and the Ottoman Empire. The Russian armies suffered a long string of defeats, resulting in the deaths of well over 1 million Russian soldiers. The war plunged the nation

Russian reserve troops were called up in late 1914 to fight in World War I.

into deeper chaos, poverty, and political upheaval. During most of the war, Lenin lived outside Russia. Following the failure of the 1905 revolution, he had been living in exile in Western Europe. In 1917, he returned to lead the Russian Revolution.

The Overthrow of the Czar

In early 1917, the Russian capital of Petrograd was in a state of disarray. Citizens protested the shortages of food and the poor working conditions. Shops closed and factories were shut down. Even the police and soldiers joined in the protests. Czar Nicholas II, realizing he had lost control of the country, stepped down from his throne. Russia's legislative body set up a temporary government in his wake. The czar and his family were captured and brought to Siberia. In July 1918, they were executed.

In the span of a few weeks in March and April 1917, Lenin and Stalin both arrived in Petrograd—Lenin from exile in Switzerland and Stalin from exile in Siberia. Lenin was a great orator and had the ability to rally crowds. His return from exile was met with thousands of Bolshevik workers and soldiers. Some in the party, including Stalin, briefly recommended the Bolsheviks align themselves with the temporary government. But Lenin encouraged a more radical stance. In the summer, the temporary government banned the Bolshevik Party, sending Lenin into hiding in Finland.

That autumn, Lenin saw his chance. He ordered the armed wing of the Bolshevik Party, the Red Guards, to attack the Winter Palace in Petrograd. This was the traditional home of the czars. In this attack, which became known

RED GUARDS

The Red Guards were armed units of workers and trained soldiers. They were the main strike force of the Bolshevik Party during the revolution and in the years following the civil war. The Red Guards eventually went on to form the Bolsheviks' Red Army during the Russian Civil War (1918–1920).

Lenin spearheaded the revolt against the Russian government and pledged to launch a worldwide socialist revolution.

as the October Revolution, Lenin and the Bolsheviks seized power from the temporary government. The new ruling party elected Lenin as their leader.

Stalin and the Revolution

Where was Stalin during the October Revolution? He had earlier proven his usefulness by gathering funds to support the Bolsheviks, and he was still a member of the party. But Stalin largely remained in the background during the revolution. He was not present at the

Bolshevik takeover of the Winter Palace. Instead, he was doing behind-the-scenes work for the revolution, setting up the newspapers needed to convince the people of the new regime's legitimacy.

Years later, when Stalin was firmly in power, he authorized biographies of himself that exaggerated his role in the revolution. In reality, however, Stalin was not at the center of the action. When Lenin returned to Russia after years of exile, Stalin claimed to be alongside him. Stalin even had photographs doctored to place himself side by side with Lenin. These deceptive techniques made Stalin appear more heroic than he actually was. Stalin's use of media in this way would later be used to maintain control over the Soviet Union. The October Revolution put Lenin, Stalin, and the Bolshevik party firmly in a position of power. Months later, they negotiated a peace with the Central powers, exiting World War I. Now, the attention of the revolutionaries turned inward.

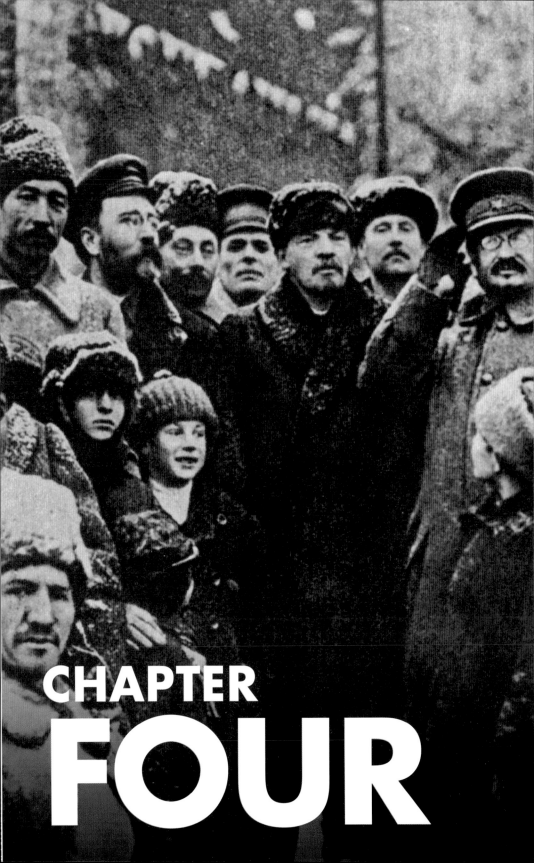

CHAPTER
FOUR

COMMUNIST RULE

U nder the firm rule of the Bolsheviks, the nation got a bitter taste of what its future held. The Bolsheviks, led by Lenin, were in control of Petrograd after the October Revolution. The Russian people were weary from years of czarist rule and the devastation of World War I. But there would be little improvement in their lives under the revolutionaries. Lenin, Stalin, Leon Trotsky, and the small group that formed the Central Committee readied themselves for a civil war that would last for several years. It would result in the rise of the Communist Party and the formation of the Union of Soviet Socialist Republics, or USSR.

After the takeover of Petrograd in the October Revolution, Lenin and his leaders formed a ruling cabinet made up of commissars. At first, they ran the nation using this cabinet, known as the Council of People's Commissars. Within a few years, the Communist Party would bypass the government and simply rule the country directly through its leadership,

Lenin, *center*, and Trotsky, *saluting*, attend a revolutionary parade in 1919.

the Central Committee. Stalin was made commissar for nationalities. In his post he would work with the non-Russian people of the new nation. Though the position did not offer immediate power, it allowed him to maneuver his way into more influence.

Lenin imposed Communism on the people of Russia. He declared that soviets, or councils of workers, would now govern the nation. He put an end to private ownership of land and took over banks. He banned private trade and businesses. Newspapers that did not support the new regime were suppressed. Lenin's new

LEON TROTSKY

Stalin's archrival Leon Trotsky was born on November 7, 1879. As a teenager, he became involved in revolutionary activities. Like many of his peers, he was arrested and sent into exile in Siberia. He later played an important role in the Russian Revolution of 1917, serving as a key military leader. Prior to the civil war, Trotsky was named war commissar, building up the powerful Red Army. Many thought he would take over following Lenin's death.

Trotsky and Stalin despised each other, and their rivalry continued after Lenin's death. Trotsky criticized the government and Stalin. But Stalin was more cunning. He took every opportunity to discredit Trotsky, formed alliances against him, and eventually exiled him. Trotsky lived in Turkey, France, and Norway before settling in Mexico. He continued to write critical articles about Stalin. On August 20, 1940, an assassin struck Trotsky in the head with an ice pick at his home in Mexico. He died a day later.

secret police force, the Cheka, hunted down political dissenters. Lenin also built up a powerful military known as the Red Army.

Civil War

Lenin, Stalin, and the leaders of the revolution soon realized opposition groups were beginning to form. One group, known as the White Army, was made up of loosely organized units from the czar's former army. The Russian Civil War began between the Bolsheviks and the anti-Communists who made up the White Army.

THE CHEKA

Lenin's police group, the Cheka, replaced the secret police group of the czar, known as the Okhrana. The ruthless Cheka imposed Lenin's policies by force and were encouraged to use brutal tactics to send a message. Their job was to hunt down, arrest, and execute the enemies of the party.

On orders from Lenin, Stalin was put in charge of the Red Army in the Caucasus, a mountain region of Russia that included his native Georgia. His job was to obtain grain from the peasants in the area and transport it to Moscow and other cities where food was in short supply. It was a job Stalin relished. He terrorized the peasants whose grain he took. He was equally ruthless toward the Red Army troops he commanded. His acts of

Red Army soldiers take aim at police forces in Petrograd.

brutality continued throughout the war years. Finally, in 1920, the civil war ended with the Communists firmly in control. White Army survivors and those who opposed the government were sent to prison, exiled, or executed. Millions of Russian citizens died during the civil war.

The Rise to Power

During the Russian Civil War, Stalin placed into power people who were loyal to him. He created spy networks to keep track of party officials. His second wife, Nadezhda Alliluyeva, was a spy in Lenin's household, where she worked as a secretary. Slowly, Stalin built up alliances. In 1922, he achieved the office of general secretary of the Communist Party's Central Committee.

Lenin became ill in 1922 and 1923, suffering strokes that paralyzed him and left him weakened. Before his death, he worked to reorganize Russia's territory into

WAR COMMUNISM

During the Russian Civil War, Lenin introduced an economic and political policy called war communism. It was a program designed to prevent the nation's economic collapse. Strikes were banned, and railways came under military control. The government took over the entire economy, and peasants were forced to give up their grain to feed others. If the peasants resisted, they were shot by Red Army firing squads.

the USSR, established in 1922. Lenin also took some steps to appease citizens disillusioned by the harsh policies of the Communists. Finally, he died in January 1924. Lenin's written instructions after his death clearly stated his criticisms of Stalin and others. With the help of his many allies throughout the government, however, Stalin was able to overcome Lenin's condemnation. Stalin turned Lenin's death into a public spectacle by having his corpse embalmed and put on public display. He attempted to associate himself closely with the deceased leader. As a result, a cult of personality began to form around Lenin and Stalin. People began to see them as powerful, heroic, and even godlike figures.

Still, Stalin shared control of the Communist Party with other powerful party members. He feared they might try to seize power. But the alliances he had established continued to pay off. He had two of his closest rivals expelled from the

NADEZHDA ALLILUYEVA

Stalin's second wife, Nadezhda Alliluyeva, was only 17 when the couple married in 1919. Together, they had two children, Vasily and Svetlana. Their marriage was not a happy one, and Stalin was frequently cruel and rude to his young wife. In 1932, distressed over the terrible famine that plagued the Soviet Union, Nadezhda shot herself.

party—only Trotsky stood in his way. In 1929, Stalin had Trotsky arrested and exiled from the Soviet Union. Years later, the fallen party member would be murdered in Mexico.

Now firmly in command of the Soviet Union, Stalin sought to transform the nation into a fully Communist society. At the same time, he sought to make the Soviet Union a great industrial power.

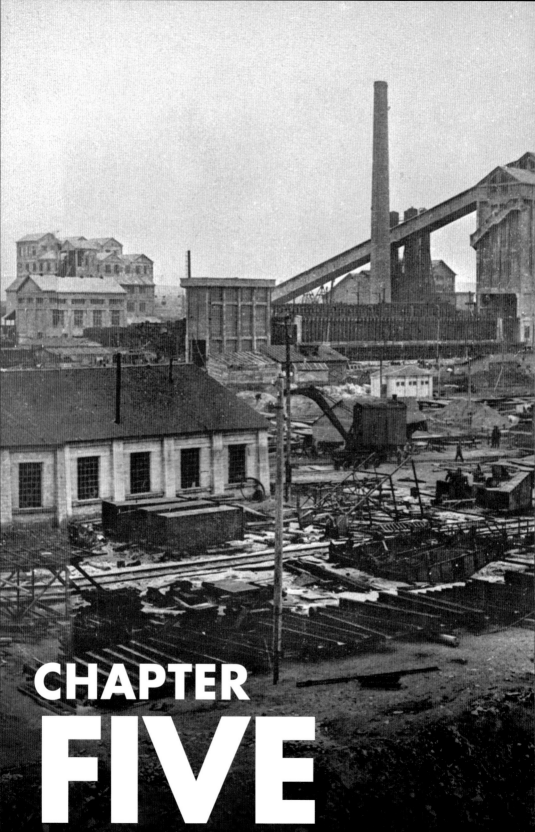

CHAPTER
FIVE

STALIN'S FIRST FIVE-YEAR PLAN

W hen Stalin took control of the Soviet Union, the country lagged behind industrial nations such as France, Germany, the United Kingdom, and the United States. But Stalin had high ambitions. He wanted to transform the country into a great industrial nation. When he rose to power, the country was made up chiefly of peasants who worked farms. Many still used animal-drawn plows. The Soviet Union did not generate nearly as much electricity as the major industrialized nations, and many of its factories were unable to produce modern machines. As a result, the Red Army's tank, airplane, and warship technology lagged behind that of other nations. Fearing stronger capitalist countries would invade the Soviet Union, Stalin came up with a plan to transform the nation. It was known as the Five-Year Plan.

The first Five-Year Plan brought huge boosts to steel, iron, and coal production.

The plan, launched in 1928, aimed to enhance the Soviet Union's heavy industry, collectivize agriculture, and build up the military. Stalin's plan put the government in control of all parts of the economy, including factories, farms, and banks. Party workers were put in charge of local economies and reported to the central government. Some Soviet citizens were forced to move to cities and work in factories, though others chose to move voluntarily. The authorities closely watched workers. If they did not meet production quotas or missed a day's work, they could be severely punished. As a result of the plan, industrial production in steel, coal, oil, electricity, and motor vehicles grew. At the same time, working conditions deteriorated.

RESULTS OF THE FIRST FIVE-YEAR PLAN

Resource	1928 Production	1932 Production
Electricity (billions of kwh)	5.0	13.5
Oil (millions of short tons)	11.6	21.4
Coal (millions of short tons)	35.5	64.4
Steel (millions of short tons)	3.4	4.4
Tractors	1,800	50,800[1]

Soviet farmers set out to collect the harvest in the autumn of 1930.

Peasants and Collective Farms

The Five-Year Plan had significant effects on Soviet peasants. Thousands of peasant-run farms were collectivized. The country's poor were still suffering from the effects of the recent civil war. Many of them were already starving. Now they were ordered to produce more grain for the state. Stalin forced peasants to organize into huge farms run by the government. These were called collective farms.

Government posters depicted the wealthy farmers as pigs.

Everything was shared within the collective farms, even mealtimes—peasants were often required to eat in large groups. Stalin's party officials closely supervised the collective farms. Those who resisted were forcibly removed from their villages, imprisoned, or simply executed. Farmers were not allowed to sell their crops for profit. Instead, they were required to sell grain to the government at fixed prices in order to feed the factory workers building Soviet heavy industry. But many farmers would not give up without a fight.

Groups of angry peasants rebelled and refused to grow grain. They slaughtered farm animals, destroyed farm machinery, and burned crops. Some even attacked party workers. But Stalin fought back, commanding his police units to suppress the peasant uprisings.

Kulaks and the Gulag

Stalin wanted to establish a classless society by eliminating the wealthier farmers, known as kulaks. In reality, however, the definition of kulak was extended to include many who opposed the state or were suspected of opposing the state. At a meeting of farmers in 1928, Stalin explained a change in policy with regard to kulaks: "From a policy of *limiting* the exploitative tendencies of the kulaks, we have gone over to a policy of *liquidating* the kulaks as a class."[2] Kulaks were exiled to remote areas of the Soviet Union or

DESTRUCTION OF THE KULAKS

The campaign against the kulaks dated back to the days of Lenin. In November 1918, he issued an order to hang a group of kulaks. In part, the order read:

You need to hang (hang without fail, so that the public sees) at least 100 notorious kulaks, the rich, and the bloodsuckers. . . . This needs to be accomplished in such a way, that people for hundreds of miles around will see, tremble, know and scream out: let's choke and strangle those blood-sucking kulaks.[3]

sent to Gulag labor camps. Others were shot and killed. Many transported to the labor camps had trials, but those exiled did not. Citizens were herded into railroad cars like cattle and shipped off. If both parents of a family were sent to the Gulag, the children were left to grandparents or other relatives or even sometimes placed in an orphanage. At the labor camps, many ordinary men and women were worked to death alongside thieves

DAILY LIFE IN THE GULAGS

Daily life in the gulags was brutal and cruel. Prisoners were wakened at an early hour and given a meager ration of food in preparation for the day's labor. Workers rarely received a day off. They often worked in temperatures as low as −40 degrees Fahrenheit (−40°C) for 10 to 12 hours a day, and sometimes longer. At the end of the workday, prisoners were forced to stand in line for up to an hour during roll call. For meals, prisoners were fed based on their work production. In one camp, daily rations of food were divided into large soup pots. Workers ate from a pot containing thin soup, bread, grain, and spoiled fish. Weak and vulnerable prisoners were doomed to death by starvation in a matter of months.

Life in the barracks was unbearable. Prisoners slept on wooden planks attached to the walls. They were given straw mattresses and thin blankets, but these did little to keep away the severe cold. Each barrack had a small stove in the corner and a pot to use as a toilet. Many prisoners were covered with lice and bites from other insects, and disease was rampant.

and murderers. Others died of starvation and the frigid cold.

Stalin used the free labor of the people in the prison camps to strengthen the Soviet economy. Imprisoned workers mined for gold and silver. They constructed highways and railroads and dug canals. They built factories and power plants. They produced goods such as car parts and furniture. But the conditions under which the people worked were often extremely harsh. Workers did not receive enough food or clothing to stay healthy and warm. Food rations depended on a worker's productivity. A worker who produced more got more food. But even those rations were meager, often barely enough to keep a worker from starving to death.

Stalin cared little about the fate of the people in these camps. To him, people were simply a resource or

EXPOSING LIFE IN THE GULAG

In the 1960s and 1970s, author Aleksandr Solzhenitsyn wrote two books exposing the horrors of life in the Gulag labor camps. Solzhenitsyn had endured eight years in prisons and labor camps after writing a letter criticizing Stalin. His books, *One Day in the Life of Ivan Denisovich*, published in the Soviet Union in 1962, and *The Gulag Archipelago*, published only abroad in 1973, became controversial in the Soviet Union and popular worldwide. After publication of *The Gulag Archipelago* abroad, Solzhenitsyn was exiled from the Soviet Union. *The Gulag Archipelago* was not allowed to be published in the Soviet Union until 1989.

Even children had to work to achieve the goals of the Five-Year Plan.

a means to an end. Peasants and factory workers—and
later, soldiers—were disposable. For every peasant who
died of starvation, there would be another to replace
him or her. Most important to Stalin were the Soviet
Union's industrialization and the maintenance of his own
power. And he would use whatever methods he needed
to achieve his goals. By 1936, historians estimate, the
population of the Gulag camps reached approximately
5 million.[4]

During this time, Stalin's focus was nearly entirely
on the politics of leading the Soviet Union. He had little

private or family life. Stalin's main social outlets were feasts for his generals and party officials. He displayed a sense of humor but usually used it to mock, tease, or ridicule his guests.

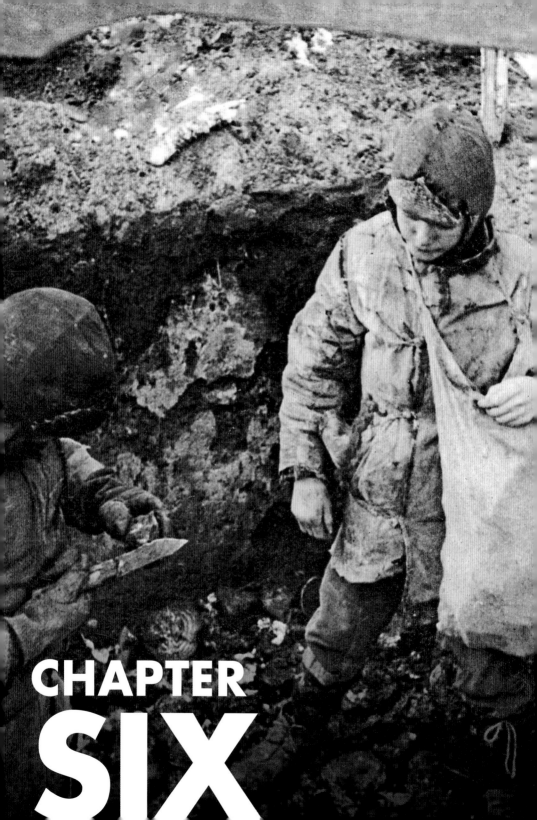

CHAPTER
SIX

PROGRESS AND SUFFERING

Stalin's Five-Year Plan achieved many of its goals. Industrial production increased. Factories were built and began operating. Workers were producing cars, tractors, tanks, and airplanes. Production at steel mills was boosted significantly. Stalin initiated huge projects intended to make the country a world superpower. Workers built the Dnieper Hydroelectric Station, which included the Dnieper Dam, the largest dam in Europe at the time. The station increased the output of electricity and lit up the countryside. Prisoners constructed a canal linking the Baltic Sea and the White Sea.

But at the same time, the Five-Year Plan had a devastating impact on millions of Soviet citizens. The collectivization and subsequent mismanagement of Soviet farms resulted in horrific famines, particularly in Ukraine and Kazakhstan. The streets of once lively villages were lined with corpses, and there were

In the midst of famine, two boys raid an elderly woman's hoard of potatoes after she is deported to Siberia.

THE HOLODOMOR

The word Holodomor comes from the Ukrainian words for "extermination by hunger." The name emphasizes the fact that many see the events as manmade rather than natural. Records show that the 1932 Ukrainian grain harvest, though below average levels, was enough to feed the country's people. Starvation resulted when Soviet officials confiscated massive amounts of grain to export, leaving little for the Ukrainians themselves. It was not until the 1980s that the Soviet Union acknowledged the existence of the famine.

reports of cannibalism. By 1933, 6 to 8 million people had died of starvation in the Soviet Union, 4 to 5 million of whom were Ukrainian.[1] Approximately 1.5 million Kazakhs also perished.[2] Some scholars and nations have recognized the famine as deliberate mass murder or even genocide, referring to it as the Holodomor.

Stalin refused to acknowledge the suffering of these millions. Newspapers and radio were forbidden to talk about the famine; reporters who raised the issue risked severe punishment. Some historians have suggested Stalin purposefully caused the famine in order to prevent peasants from rising up against the government.

A Totalitarian Dictator

By the early 1930s, Stalin was a totalitarian dictator with iron control over the Soviet Union. He built and maintained his grip on power by continuing to surround himself with officials loyal to him personally. Those suspected of opposing him were eliminated.

Stalin organized the People's Commissariat for Internal Affairs, or the NKVD, in 1934. This group was one of the successors to Lenin's Cheka security force. The NKVD was Stalin's secret police. It backed Stalin and ruthlessly silenced dissenters. A person could be arrested and jailed without a trial. People could be questioned and tortured without cause. And if a person was perceived to be a threat to the state, he or she could be summarily executed. Soviet citizens were also forbidden to leave the country. If a person did manage to escape, his or her family could be subjected to severe punishment.

EDUCATION UNDER STALIN

In the early 1900s, Russia was a land of illiterate peasants. But Stalin built schools and sent Soviet children to school. Under Stalin, the literacy rate rose to be equal to that of Western countries. Students learned mathematics, read literature, and studied science. But there was little freedom of thought or expression in the schools, and propaganda was commonplace.

Stalin gave a dramatic speech about collective farming in 1935.

Propaganda

Stalin ruled by fear and brute force. But he also created a heroic image of himself through propaganda. After Lenin died, Stalin worked to glorify the dead leader. By doing so, he began to associate himself with Lenin's accomplishments. He rewrote history in official biographies, placing himself at Lenin's side when he had actually been elsewhere. He glorified himself by erecting statues and placing huge pictures of himself in cities all over the Soviet Union. He even changed the name of the city Tsaritsyn to Stalingrad.

Through propaganda, Stalin made himself appear to be a benevolent leader. Drawing on his experience editing newspapers during the Russian Revolution, he

TOTALITARIAN DICTATORS OF THE TWENTIETH CENTURY

The twentieth century saw the rise of the most notorious totalitarian dictators in history. Along with Stalin, they included Benito Mussolini of Italy and Adolf Hitler of Germany. Mussolini would impose an extreme form of nationalism known as fascism on the Italian people. Hitler brought about the rise of Nazi Germany, igniting World War II, during which he was allied with Mussolini against Stalin. The Nazis under Hitler exterminated millions of people in their infamous concentration camps. Both Mussolini and Hitler were dead by the end of World War II.

controlled the press and what was written about him. The industrialization and modernization of their nation, coupled with a heavy dose of propaganda, led many Soviet citizens to believe in Stalin's wisdom as a leader. The propaganda drew attention toward the progress made in the Five-Year Plan and away from the crimes he committed against his own people.

STALIN AND THE ARTS

Stalin believed the arts should support his ideas. In his attempt to control the arts, Stalin forced artists and writers to use a style of art that became known as socialist realism. This type of "realism" was not intended to show the world as it really was but as it was supposed to be. Thus, Communism was always portrayed in a positive light. Artists were forced to paint pictures of a glorious Soviet Union. Paintings of factories and collective farms were intended to praise the accomplishments of the Five-Year Plan. Many paintings showed happy, hardworking peasants in their collective farms. The paintings were far from the truth. Artists also were required to paint pictures of Stalin himself to enhance his godlike image. Paintings frequently included the hammer and sickle, the symbol of the Soviet Union.

Writers and musicians also had to depict a thriving Communist society. The state controlled which books were published. Musicians had to write music that was uplifting and inspirational. Artists, writers, and musicians were not allowed to criticize the government through their works. Those who did not follow Stalin's strict rules were given punishments ranging from the loss of state funding to imprisonment to exile. The arts became another tool of propaganda for Stalin.

Giant portraits in public spaces aimed to glorify
Stalin in the eyes of the Soviet people.

CHAPTER
SEVEN

THE GREAT TERROR

Stalin was a paranoid person who constantly suspected people of plotting against him. Communism itself was a paranoid belief system that presumed the existence of internal and external enemies bent on destruction of the socialist state. As Stalin rose, he and the other leaders of the Soviet Union became more suspicious of everyone, including each other. This environment of paranoia would lead the Soviet people into one of the most frightening periods in Soviet history. Stalin knew many people both in the Communist Party and outside the government feared and hated him. He began working to destroy anyone who he felt could oppose him. This period began in 1934 and lasted until 1939. It became known among historians as the Great Terror.

The 1934 assassination of party member Sergey Kirov gave Stalin the excuse he needed to begin large-scale purges of political opponents. Kirov was a popular, charismatic, and powerful member of

Stalin, *center,* **at the funeral of Sergey Kirov**

After being executed, Stalin's enemies were sometimes even removed from official photographs.

the Communist Party. Historians later came to the conclusion that Stalin was likely not responsible for Kirov's murder. In any event, with a major member of the Communist Party dead, Stalin now had the opportunity to strike back at any and all of his political enemies.

The murder of Kirov set off a series of purges that resulted in the executions of 98 of the 139 members of the Central Committee.[1] Stalin accused some party leaders of the assassination. They were promptly arrested. Even old Bolsheviks who had spearheaded the revolution of 1917 were arrested and executed. When it was over, Stalin had effectively eliminated anyone who could challenge his leadership.

During this time, Stalin also used the NKVD, led by Nikolai Yezhov, to target workers, peasants, writers, artists, scientists, and other ordinary citizens. He intended to purge the Soviet Union of anyone and everyone who could be a political rival or enemy of the state. The result was terror and bloodshed. Millions were executed, exiled,

ERASED FROM THE RECORDS

Stalin appointed Nikolai Yezhov as leader of the NKVD in 1936. Yezhov led the secret police in purging party members and other innocent victims. When he had outlived his usefulness, Stalin had Yezhov arrested, tortured, and executed. Stalin would later erase his name from the records. He rewrote the official histories to delete evidence of Yezhov's activities.

or sent to Gulag camps during this reign of terror. As the scope of the violence widened, Soviet citizens realized that no one was exempt from the purge.

Stalin's spies and secret police were everywhere. A Soviet citizen could never know if a trusted neighbor or coworker was an informant for the government. When wives and children said goodbye to husbands and fathers in the morning, they could never be sure if they would ever see each other again. The NKVD arrested people on suspicion alone. A person could be held and interrogated for hours or even days without lawyers or counsel. Citizens were terrorized, tortured, or blackmailed into making false confessions or naming other supposed conspirators against the state. NKVD police had the power to sentence anyone to death without a trial. Guards often executed people right on the spot. There was a climate of fear everywhere, and few dared to question Stalin.

Lavrenty Beria became the most notorious head of the NKVD.

The Party and the Military

Stalin targeted the very people who had helped him rise
to power. The Bolsheviks who had brought about the
revolution were now suspected of counterrevolution.
Some party members were beginning to tire of

Stalin, *top left*, reviews a military parade with top Soviet officials in 1937. Within two years, four of the officials pictured were dead.

Stalin's harsh demands. Others grumbled about the disastrous effects of the Five-Year Plan. Stalin knew some party members were not happy with his methods, and he proceeded to purge the party of these suspected enemies.

Fear spread like wildfire through party members. No person was safe from Stalin. Even family members of party officials were at risk. People were encouraged to turn in anyone suspected of being against the Communist Party. Husbands and wives turned each other in, and children were encouraged to tell the authorities if they heard their parents speaking out against Stalin and his regime.

Stalin's own military was another of his targets. He felt admirals, generals, and other military leaders could also be a threat to his rule. Stalin accused Red Army officials of plotting against him with foreign powers. Military officers suffered the same fate as the Bolsheviks and party officials. Many were arrested on false charges and executed. By the time Stalin was finished with his military purge, 81 of the Soviet Union's 103 generals and admirals had been executed.[2] The purge would have a devastating effect on the Soviet Union's ability to defend itself.

STALIN'S ORPHANS

During the Great Terror, many children lost both parents to execution, prison camps, or exile. Children who did not have close relatives were placed in orphanages. Many of these children were given new names by government workers. This was so the children could not remember their real names and discover what had happened to their parents.

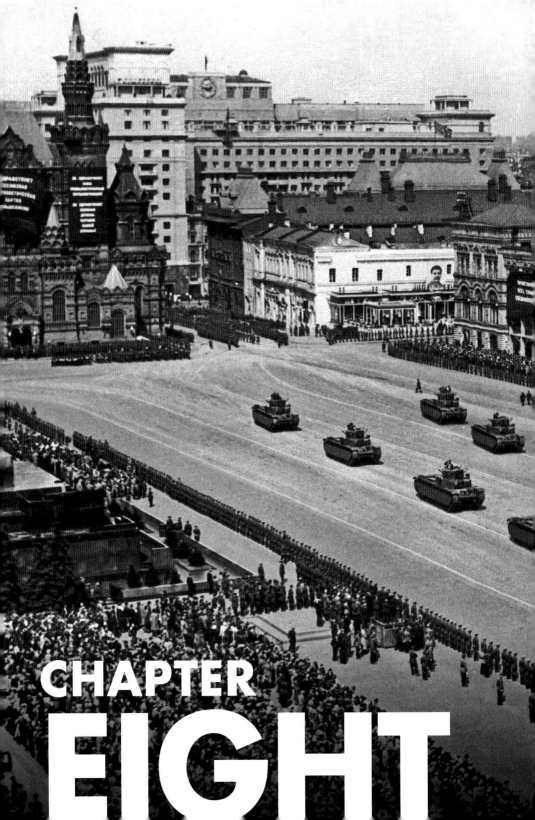

CHAPTER
EIGHT

WORLD WAR II

B y the time of Stalin's Great Terror, dictators had risen to power in Italy and Germany. Benito Mussolini, who was in complete control of Italy by 1925, ruled with a firm hand and used violence to maintain his power. Adolf Hitler had become the leader of Germany by 1934. Both ruled under a political system known as fascism, which favored a strong national state ruled by a dictator. Italy and Germany were suffering the effects of economic depression, and their citizens looked for strong leaders to create jobs and improve their lives.

Hitler's Nazi Party lifted a poverty-stricken country out of its economic chaos. Like Stalin, he did so with little regard for his people. He built powerful war industries to produce modern tanks and airplanes. Hitler's goal was to conquer Europe and populate it with what he considered the superior race of German people. He sought to control every aspect of his people's lives and exceeded even Stalin in his cruel and inhuman

Wary of the rise of dictators in Europe, Stalin built up his military in the late 1930s.

policies, murdering many millions of Jewish, Slavic, and Roma people, among others, during his reign.

Hitler also hated Communists. His ambitions startled Stalin, who recognized Hitler's thirst for power. Stalin knew of Hitler's ruthless desire to expand his empire, which included land belonging to the Soviet Union. Stalin watched and waited, observing Hitler and his actions quietly from afar. He knew war would come eventually. He also knew the Soviet Union was not prepared for war. The execution or exile of generals and admirals during the Great Terror left the Soviet military in the hands of inexperienced leaders. Only the country of Poland stood between Hitler's Germany and Stalin's Soviet Union.

Hitler wanted to invade Poland, but he also wanted to delay the inevitable conflict against Stalin. So Hitler offered Stalin a deal. In August 1939, the two powers signed a nonaggression pact agreeing not to go to war with each other. They also agreed to divide conquered territory in Poland between them. One week later, Hitler's army invaded Poland. In response, Polish allies France and the United Kingdom declared war on Germany. World War II had begun. On September 17, Stalin's forces invaded Poland from the East. Many Poles

After the Polish military quickly collapsed, Nazi troops poured by the thousands into Poland—and onto Stalin's border.

were sent to Stalin's prison camps, and Polish military officers were arrested. In the infamous Katyn Massacre, the NKVD executed more than 20,000 Polish prisoners of war in early 1940.[1] The fate of the Poles in the East was often as gruesome as the fate of the Poles caught in Hitler's war machine.

Hitler Invades the Soviet Union

In the year following Hitler's invasion of Poland, the German dictator conquered Denmark, Norway,

The Nazi attack on the Soviet Union in 1941 was the largest invasion in world history.

Belgium, Luxembourg, and France. He launched a major aerial attack on the United Kingdom. With the signing of the Tripartite Pact in September 1940, Hitler formally allied himself with Japan and Italy. The three nations became known as the Axis powers.

Stalin knew an attack on the Soviet Union would come eventually. But against evidence to the contrary, he did not believe Hitler would break their pact so soon. Soviet spies in Germany repeatedly warned him about the buildup of Nazi forces near the Soviet border. Still, he failed to fully mobilize the Red Army. When the attack came, Stalin was unprepared.

Operation Barbarossa, Hitler's invasion of the Soviet Union, was launched in June 1941. The consequences were devastating to the Soviets. Hitler's forces marched through the country like lightning. Some citizens thought Hitler's forces would finally release them from Stalin's terrible oppression. But they were wrong. The German troops were brutal to captured Red Army soldiers and civilians alike. Within a few months, more than 1 million Germans and Soviets were dead.[2] By December, German forces were close enough to the Soviet Union's capital, Moscow, they could see it through binoculars.

Stalin would not let the country he had built go down without a fight. He refused to leave Moscow as German forces drew nearer. He inspired a surge of patriotism, and the Soviet people rose up to defend their country. Stalin ordered a military

HITLER ON STALIN

Hitler knew Stalin had as little regard for human life as he did. He also knew Stalin was equally ruthless. Soon after Operation Barbarossa began, Hitler observed, "Stalin is one of the most extraordinary figures in human history. . . . [He] is apparently quite ready to abandon European Russia, if he thinks that a failure to solve her problems would cause him to lose everything."[3]

parade through Moscow. The soldiers marched past cheering crowds and directly to the battlefield. Factories were taken apart piece by piece, moved hundreds of miles east, and rebuilt. Soviet soldiers destroyed bridges and military equipment as they retreated, and peasants destroyed crops to prevent them from falling into German hands. The Red Army fought fiercely and held its ground near Moscow. After months of fighting, the

STALIN'S RED ARMY

The soldiers of Stalin's Red Army were under strict orders to never surrender. To do so was considered an act of treason. Stalin expected every soldier to fight to the death, so he believed any soldier who was captured alive or escaped from capture was a traitor. Still, approximately 5.7 million of his soldiers fell into enemy hands during the war. Hitler targeted these prisoners of war for death because of his racial policies, believing them to be subhuman. More than half of the Soviet prisoners taken by the Nazis died in captivity. By comparison, less than 4 percent of British and American prisoners of war died in Nazi custody.[4]

But the ordeal of Soviet prisoners of war did not end with their release after Germany's surrender. Because he had declared that these soldiers were traitors, Stalin imprisoned many of them in the Gulag or simply had them shot outright. Stalin's own son, Yakov, was a Red Army soldier. Early in the war, the Germans took him prisoner. Stalin's daughter later revealed that the Germans offered to trade Yakov for German prisoners. But Stalin refused, declaring, "I have no son named Yakov."[5]

combined force of the Red Army and the brutal Russian winter brought the German attack to a standstill.

The Nazis were beaten back slowly at the cost of many lives. Hundreds of thousands died on each side in the major battles. Stalin held little regard for the lives of his soldiers. Men were repeatedly ordered into frontal assaults on Nazi positions with the knowledge that the vast majority of attackers would surely die. The brutality did not end there. In an August 1941 order, Stalin commanded, "Anyone who removes his insignia during battle and surrenders should be regarded as a malicious deserter, whose family is to be arrested. . . . Such deserters are to be shot on the spot."[6] Stalin's NKVD forces stood behind the front lines, ready to machine-gun any Soviet soldiers who dared retreat. More than 150,000 were executed for desertion.[7]

The Allies

In order to defeat the Germans, Stalin entered into an alliance with the United States and the United Kingdom. The nations became known as the Allies. The United States had been drawn into the war by Japan's infamous attack on Pearl Harbor, Hawaii, on December 7, 1941. Soon after, Hitler declared war

In November 1943 Stalin, *left*, met with Roosevelt, *center*, and Churchill, *right*, to make plans for the postwar period.

on the United States. In November 1943, Stalin met with President Franklin D. Roosevelt of the United States and Prime Minister Winston Churchill of the United Kingdom. The three leaders met in Tehran, the capital of Iran, to discuss war plans. Stalin's decision to align himself with capitalist countries went against his Communist beliefs. But the three leaders all had one thing in common: they needed to stop Hitler. The alliance was shaky at best. Churchill was wary of Stalin but was impressed with his grasp of military strategies.

Roosevelt was optimistic Stalin could work with the other Allies to achieve world peace, but some of his advisers were much more skeptical of the Communist leader. Stalin was suspicious of Churchill and Roosevelt, believing they were intentionally delaying the opening of a second front in Europe to allow the Nazis to weaken the Soviets. Together, the three men decided how to finish off Hitler. Roosevelt and Churchill granted major concessions to Stalin, allowing him to take possession of some territories the Red Army passed through on the way to Germany. This decision would have a major impact on the postwar world.

The Allies were planning an invasion of France to break Hitler's stranglehold on Western Europe and to relieve pressure on Stalin's forces in the East. After incredibly costly victories at Stalingrad, Kursk, and Leningrad, Stalin's Red Army was beginning to drive the Germans out of the Soviet Union.

MAN OF THE YEAR

Time magazine declared Stalin the Man of the Year of 1942 for his role in the war. Its editorial page declared: "The man whose name means steel in Russian, whose few words of English include the American expression 'tough guy' was the man of 1942. Only Joseph Stalin fully knew how close Russia stood to defeat in 1942, and only Joseph Stalin knew how he brought Russia through."[8]

On June 6, 1944—commonly known as D-Day—a massive Allied invasion of Western Europe was launched from the United Kingdom. The surprise attack on the shores of Normandy, France, finally opened the second front Stalin had been asking for. In the ensuing months, Allied forces fought their way through Europe toward Germany from both the east and west. The Soviets reached the German capital of Berlin first. With the Red Army just miles from his underground bunker, Hitler killed himself. The Nazis surrendered days later, ending the war in Europe.

THE DEADLIEST WAR IN HISTORY

More people died during World War II than in any other conflict in human history. Between September 1939 and August 1945, an average of 27,000 people died per day as a result of the war.[9] The Soviet Union suffered the most by far. Some 26 million soldiers and civilians were killed and tens of thousands of towns, cities, and villages were destroyed.[10]

Still, the Allies' war against Japan raged in the East. Fulfilling a promise he had made to Roosevelt, Stalin ordered his forces to invade Japanese territory in mainland Asia on August 9, 1945. That same day, the United States dropped the second of two atomic bombs on Japan, vaporizing much of the city of Nagasaki. Three days later, Japan surrendered. World War II was over.

From the time Hitler invaded the Soviet Union until the final surrender of Japan, approximately 26 million of Stalin's countrymen had died from an initial population of approximately 130 million.[11] Though the prewar industrialization of the nation had proven devastating for many Soviet citizens, it had also boosted production efficiency and technological developments. Without Stalin's modernization program, the Soviet Union could not have won the war. War had destroyed much of the Soviet Union, but its territorial gains and booming war economy set it up to become a major power. It was becoming clear the postwar world would be dominated by the rivalry between the Soviet Union and the United States.

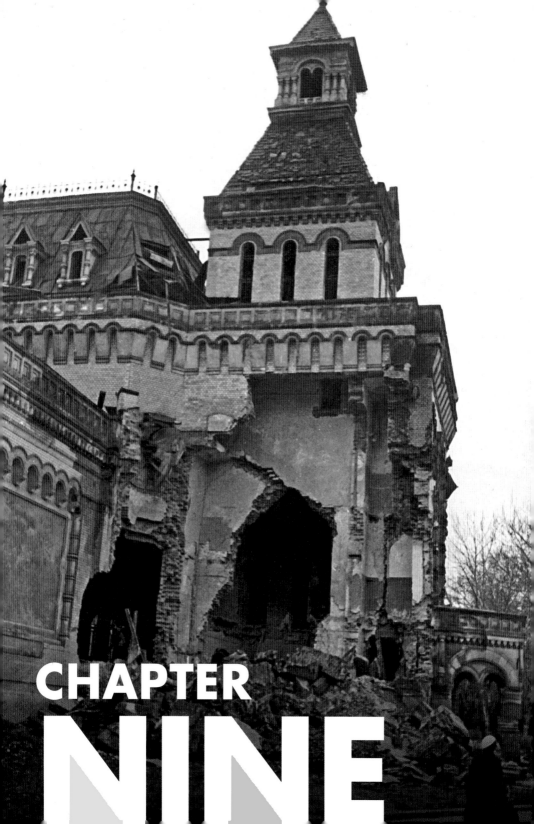

CHAPTER
NINE

THE IRON CURTAIN DESCENDS

World War II changed the course of history, and Stalin was quick to ensure these changes served his ambitions. A few months before the war's end, Stalin once again met with Churchill and Roosevelt. The so-called Big Three met in 1945 at Yalta, Ukraine, on the Black Sea. Their task was to set up a lasting peace agreement in war-torn Europe. But Stalin had his own ideas. He aimed to win more territory for the Soviet Union. His former allies during the war now became rivals.

After the war, the Soviet Union continued to occupy the countries where it had fought the Nazis. These included Czechoslovakia, Hungary, Romania, Bulgaria, East Germany, the eastern half of Poland, and the Baltic States of Estonia, Latvia, and Lithuania. Both Churchill and Roosevelt wanted to ensure democratic elections in the occupied countries. But Stalin expected to extract a

World War II left much of the Soviet Union in ruins.

reward for his nation's sacrifice. He set up Communist regimes in the occupied countries, and the German capital of Berlin was split down the middle. The Soviet Union controlled the eastern half, and the other Allies controlled the western half.

The newly Communist countries formed a Communist buffer zone between the Soviet Union and the Western democracies. The occupied countries became satellites of the Soviet Union. The people of these countries had initially welcomed the Soviet troops as liberators from Nazi control. But they soon realized the Communist rule over their countries was little better than that of the Nazis.

The governments in the satellite countries were supposedly independent, but in reality Stalin exerted tight control over them. Those who opposed Communist rule were imprisoned or executed. Private properties and businesses were taken over by the government. Stalin rigged elections and put supporters in charge. With the help of the Red Army and the NKVD, Stalin was able to crush opposition in both the Soviet Union and in the satellites. In a famous speech in 1946, Winston Churchill expressed his dismay over what Stalin had done, saying "A shadow has fallen upon the scenes so lately lighted by the Allied victory. . . . an iron curtain has descended across the Continent."[1]

Cold War and Propaganda

In the postwar period, the Soviet Union emerged as a world superpower opposite the United States. The rivalry between them became known as the Cold War. This conflict pitted the United States and other capitalist countries against the Soviet Union and the Communist countries it controlled. The two rival superpowers never actually went to war directly with each other, but they competed to spread their influence across the globe. Stalin did much to encourage this tension between the Soviet Union and the United States. At the same time, people in the United States were subject to propaganda depicting Communism and the Soviet Union as evil forces, heightening the tension even further.

Churchill coined the phrase *iron curtain* in a speech
at Westminster College in Missouri.

Stalin was determined to turn his people against all capitalist countries, especially the United States. He employed propaganda to control what the Soviet people thought about capitalism and capitalist nations. He used media to present highly selective truths and distortions about the United States, making Soviet citizens believe Americans were enemies. He controlled newspapers, magazines, books, radio, and television. They all had to portray the United States as a country that would use its power and wealth to crush the Soviet Union. In 1947, he even made it illegal for Soviet citizens to marry foreigners.

A Soviet Superpower

With the country in ruins following World War II, there was a great deal of repair and construction needed. The Soviet Union again boosted its heavy industries. Stalin's propaganda—along with the NKVD—convinced Soviet citizens to make sacrifices. Consumer goods such as clothes,

COLD WAR PROPAGANDA

Propaganda posters appeared all over the Soviet Union during the Cold War. Some posters showed Uncle Sam, the symbol of the United States, as a warmonger clutching handfuls of money. Others showed Winston Churchill as a drooling old man. The posters often showed stern Soviet soldiers warning Uncle Sam and Churchill to stay away.

Да здравствует великий вождь и учитель коммунистической партии и советского народа товарищ И. В. Сталин !

Communist leaders gathered to commemorate Stalin's seventieth birthday.

cars, and common household items were given low priority. Stalin launched a new Five-Year Plan in 1945 to increase production of steel, oil, and coal. Industries grew, and the manufacture of railroads, planes, and machinery increased. So did the production of weapons, including atomic bombs.

For several years prior to the atomic bombing of Nagasaki, the United States had been working to create atomic bombs. The effort was known as the Manhattan Project. By the summer of 1945, the project was nearing its goal. At a wartime conference in Yalta, Ukraine,

President Harry S. Truman hinted to Stalin that the United States would soon possess a new and unusual weapon. Stalin was reportedly unimpressed. In fact, Stalin had long been aware of the atomic bomb, thanks to Soviet spies in the Manhattan Project. Soviet scientists were already hard at work creating an atomic bomb of their own. By the late 1940s, the nuclear arms race was on. The Soviet Union tested its first atomic bomb in 1949. That same year, Stalin celebrated his seventieth birthday.

In the years following World War II, cracks began to show in the Soviet Union's new empire. Yugoslavia, one of the nations liberated by the Soviet Union and subsequently turned into a satellite, broke with Stalin in 1948 and sought to become independent. The Western nations took advantage of this, backing Yugoslavia and sending its people aid. Furious over the betrayal, Stalin launched

THE YALTA CONFERENCE

The Yalta Conference covered several key points dealing with the end and aftermath of the war. Stalin agreed to attack Japan within 90 days of Germany's defeat, and German civilians would be deported to the Soviet Union for the purpose of forced labor as a form of war reparations. These two points came to fruition, but Stalin also promised to allow free elections in Poland—a promise he never fulfilled.

more purges in the satellite countries. Leaders who confessed to disloyalty were executed.

Stalin became more and more paranoid over time. In 1952, he accused a group of Jewish doctors of secretly working to shorten the lives of Soviet officials. Historians have suggested he planned another round of show trials and purges. But on March 5, 1953, Stalin's response to the so-called Doctor's Plot was prevented by his death.

STALIN'S DAUGHTER

Svetlana Alliluyeva was Stalin's only daughter. She wrote her memories of her father in two books, *Only One Year* and *Twenty Letters to a Friend*. Svetlana remembers her childhood as happy. She recalls a playful father and a home filled with friends and family. But as she grew older, Stalin grew suspicious of her and rejected her because she married a Jewish man. Alliluyeva witnessed her father's death in 1953. In 1967, she left the Soviet Union and moved to the United States. About Stalin's demise, she wrote:

"The death agony was horrible. He literally choked to death as we watched. At what seemed like the very last moment he suddenly opened his eyes and cast a glance over everyone in the room. It was a terrible glance, insane or perhaps angry and full of fear of death. . . . He suddenly lifted his left hand as though he were pointing to something above and bringing a curse on us all. The gesture was . . . full of menace, and no one could say to whom or at what it might be directed."[2]

Stalin's daughter remembered her early years with her father fondly.

A few nights earlier, his household staff became suspicious when he did not emerge from his bedroom by 9:30 p.m. No one was allowed into his room without permission, so they were hesitant to enter. Finally, at 11:00 p.m., one of his guards entered Stalin's bedroom. The general secretary of the Communist Party of the Soviet Union was lying on the floor, struggling to raise his hand and speak. He had suffered a serious stroke and soon lost consciousness. Stalin was dead four days later.

CHAPTER
TEN

A DARK LEGACY

A coffin draped in black and red silk carried Stalin's body in his funeral procession on March 9, 1953. Stalin had inflicted decades of misery upon many Soviet people. But at the same time, he had modernized the country and turned it into a world superpower. He had led the nation to victory in the deadliest war in human history. Remembering these parts of his legacy, many Soviet citizens mourned his death. A massive crowd swarmed to watch the funeral procession in Red Square. In some areas, the crowds were so dense that people were crushed to death. Stalin's body was put on display for three days. Huge crowds came to pay respects to the dead leader. He was placed next to Lenin in the mausoleum. Thousands came and wept at his grave. Citizens of the Soviet Union saw Stalin as a powerful leader who dramatically improved the standing of their country. However, not everyone mourned his passing. Many were relieved at the news

Stalin's body was put on public display, where it was visited by thousands of mourners.

of his death, especially political opponents—whether suspected or actual.

Stalin's last months were tragic and ugly. He held long drinking parties at the Kremlin, the official residence of the leader of the Soviet Union. At the parties, he would play cruel jokes on party leaders. Most of his family had died, been jailed, or left the country. He was alone and more paranoid and suspicious than ever, trusting no one. The NKVD even feared he would turn on them, but continued to do his bidding anyway. His house had locks, barricades, and bars to prevent anyone from entering. He even had his food tested for poison. During this time he was heard to remark, "I'm finished. I trust no one, not even myself."[1]

The Secret Speech

In 1956, Stalin's successor Nikita Khrushchev made a historic speech to the members of the twentieth Congress of the Communist Party. The speech was called "On the Cult of Personality and Its Consequences," but it later became known as the Secret Speech because it was given in a secret session. Thousands of Communist Party members were present, but the speech was not intended for the public. Khrushchev explained the ways in which Stalin had built a cult of personality around himself. He also noted that doing so ran counter to the teachings of Marxism-Leninism. Essentially, Khrushchev was charging Stalin with the abuse of his power and a betrayal of Lenin. The party members who listened to Khrushchev's speech were stunned. Any person who had spoken out about Stalin in this way when he was alive would surely have been sentenced to death. But now it opened the door for changes in the Soviet Union.

NIKITA KHRUSHCHEV

Nikita Khrushchev was the leader of the Soviet Union from 1953 to 1964. Khrushchev was one of Stalin's party members, and he had been present at the Battle of Stalingrad during World War II. Although he eased up on Stalin's harsh policies, he still believed Communism would eventually crush capitalism. In 1964, the members of the Central Committee forced him to retire. He published his memoir *Khrushchev Remembers* in 1970 and died the next year.

Khrushchev's de-Stalinization process brought significant changes to the Soviet Union.

Khrushchev put into place a process known as de-Stalinization. This process was meant to purge the Soviet Union of Stalin and his crimes. Khrushchev freed some political prisoners and eased up on censorship. Statues and paintings of Stalin were removed. Within a few years, Stalingrad was renamed Volgograd. Still, the Communist state Stalin helped create would remain in existence for the next three decades.

A Nation Dissolves

Over the years, more of the truth about Stalin's murderous rampages has been revealed. In 1987, Soviet leader Mikhail Gorbachev closed down the Gulag.

People who were freed began to tell their stories in writings and paintings and gave accounts of the terrible horrors of the labor camps. Mass graves were discovered where thousands of men, women, children, or soldiers were buried. These graves had been hidden for many years. Once revealed, they became potent evidence of the slayings carried out by the Red Army and Stalin's NKVD police.

The Soviet Union began to break apart in 1989 when many of its republics declared their independence.

THE MASS GRAVE AT KOLPASHEVO

Kolpashevo is a tiny village on the Russian and Mongolian border. In May 1979, the banks of the Ob River, which passes by the tiny town, became exposed by erosion. As the water washed away the river's banks, it exposed a horror buried there for decades—thousands of human skeletons. Buried beneath the crumbling bones was another layer of human corpses. The bodies had been buried in the dry sand and were preserved by the cold. Most had bullet holes in their heads. But the townspeople of Kolpashevo knew why the bodies were there. Some even recognized the bodies of people they had known. This tiny town had been the home of an NKVD office in the 1930s. Stalin's notorious secret police executed these people during Stalin's Great Terror.

At first, the Communist leaders tried to hide that these bodies were Stalin's victims. The KGB, the new Soviet secret police, rushed to the town. They roped off the area and would not allow any pictures to be taken. They tried to cover up the evidence by sinking the bodies in the river. But their attempts failed. Word began to leak out about the mass grave. The victims of Kolpashevo are a grim reminder of the grisly policies of Stalin.

A leader of the modern Russian Communist Party
lays a wreath on Stalin's grave in 2004.

Then, in December 1991, the country dissolved into a
loosely affiliated group of nations known collectively as
the Commonwealth of Independent States. The largest
member was the Russian Federation. Stalin's empire
ceased to exist. Today, the Russian Federation has an
officially democratic government and is a free-market
capitalist country. However, Russia still suffers from
corruption in its government and crackdowns on
free speech.

Stalin left a dark and complex legacy. Modern
historians still work to understand him. Millions of

innocent people were murdered, starved, and exiled as direct and indirect results of his harsh policies. It is impossible to know the exact figures. But Stalin also turned the Soviet Union from a nation of peasants into an industrial superpower. During World War II, his country bore the brunt of the Nazi assault. His alliance with the United States and the United Kingdom helped defeat Hitler. Stalin looms large more than half a century after his death.

STALIN'S GRAVE

Stalin was initially embalmed and placed in the same mausoleum as Lenin. But as part of the de-Stalinization process, Nikita Khrushchev decided to move the body to another resting place. It was determined Stalin was not worthy of burial next to Lenin, and his body was quietly reburied behind the Kremlin on October 31, 1961. A stone monument marks his grave.

TIMELINE

1878
Joseph Djugashvili is born on December 6 in Gori, a village in the Russian territory of Georgia.

1894
Joseph enters seminary to study for the priesthood.

1899
Joseph is expelled from seminary and begins the life of a revolutionary.

1904
Joseph marries his first wife, Ekaterina Svanidze.

1905
Stalin meets Vladimir Lenin for the first time in Finland.

1914
World War I begins. It proves disastrous for Russia.

1917

Nicholas II steps down from his throne, and a temporary government is formed; Lenin and the Bolsheviks seize power in the Russian Revolution. The Russian Civil War begins soon after.

1919

Stalin marries his second wife, Nadezhda Alliluyeva.

1920

The Russian Civil War ends with the Red Army's victory.

1924

On January 21, Lenin dies and Stalin begins to take control of the Communist Party.

1928

Stalin launches the first Five-Year Plan, resulting in the deaths of millions.

1932

Stalin's wife commits suicide.

TIMELINE

1934

Stalin organizes the NKVD. The Great Terror begins.

1939

Germany invades Poland in September, igniting World War II.

1940

Leon Trotsky is assassinated in Mexico.

1941

On June 22, Nazi Germany invades the Soviet Union.

1943

Stalin meets with Winston Churchill and Franklin D. Roosevelt in Tehran to plan their strategy against Adolf Hitler.

1945

The Allies defeat Nazi Germany and World War II ends.

1948

Yugoslavia severs relations with the Soviet Union, infuriating Stalin.

1949

The Soviet Union tests its first atomic bomb.

1953

On March 5, Joseph Stalin dies of a stroke.

1956

Nikita Khrushchev holds his Secret Speech denouncing Stalin for his crimes. De-Stalinization begins.

1961

On October 31, Stalin's body is moved to its final resting place near the Kremlin.

ESSENTIAL FACTS

Date of Birth
December 6, 1878

Place of Birth
Gori, Georgia

Date of Death
March 5, 1953

Parents
Vissarion Djugashvili and Ekaterina Djugashvili

Education
Tiflis Spiritual Seminary

Marriage
Ekaterina Svanidze (1904–1907)
Nadezhda Alliluyeva (1919–1932)

Children
Yakov, Vasily, Svetlana

Historical Significance

Stalin took part in the Russian Revolution in 1917 that established Communist rule in the Soviet Union. By 1929, he had crushed his opposition and was firmly in place as dictator. His Five-Year Plan and collectivization campaigns resulted in mass famine and led to the deaths of millions. At the same time, his focus on boosting the nation's heavy industry modernized the Soviet Union and brought it up to par with other world powers. In 1934, he began a campaign of terror to eliminate his perceived enemies. Working with the United States and the United Kingdom, he led the Soviet Union against the Germans in World War II. His subsequent takeover of Eastern European countries led to the Cold War. In the process, Stalin further industrialized and modernized the Soviet Union, making it a world superpower with a powerful military.

Quote

"I'm finished. I trust no one, not even myself."—*Joseph Stalin*

GLOSSARY

capitalism
An economic system in which factories, services, and goods are privately owned.

collectivization
The process of forcing peasants to live and work on huge farms known as collective farms.

commissar
A Communist official in the former Soviet Union responsible for political education and organization.

Communism
An economic system based on the elimination of private ownership of factories, land, and other means of economic production.

exile
To banish a person from his or her homeland.

famine
A widespread lack of food resulting in hunger and starvation.

kulak
A rich peasant farmer in Russia who was persecuted severely during collectivization.

Marxism-Leninism
A form of Communism in which a political party seizes power and controls the economy.

propaganda
Information intended to promote a particular political cause or point of view.

reparation
The payment for damages done.

satellite
A smaller nation controlled by a larger nation.

soviet
A revolutionary council of workers or peasants.

totalitarianism
The absolute rule of a dictator or military government.

ADDITIONAL RESOURCES

Selected Bibliography

Medvedev, Zhores, and Roy Medvedev. *The Unknown Stalin*. Trans. Ellen Dahrendorf. New York: I. B. Tauris, 2003. Print.

Montefiore, Simon Sebag. *Young Stalin*. New York: Alfred A. Knopf, 2007. Print.

Service, Robert. *Stalin: A Biography*. Cambridge, MA: Harvard UP, 2004. Print.

Further Readings

McCollum, Sean. *Stalin (A Wicked History)*. New York: Franklin Watts, 2010. Print.

Pelleschi, Andrea. *Russia*. Minneapolis, MN: Abdo, 2013. Print.

Websites

To learn more about Essential Lives, visit **booklinks.abdopublishing.com**. These links are routinely monitored and updated to provide the most current information available.

Places to Visit

The Museum of Russian Art
5500 Stevens Avenue South
Minneapolis, Minnesota
612-821-9045
http://tmora.org
Explore Russian art from the twentieth century, including works of Socialist Realism.

The Winter Palace
32-38 Dvortsovaia Naberezhnaia
Saint Petersburg, Russia
http://www.saint-petersburg.com/virtual-tour/hermitage.asp
Visit a key site in the Russian Revolution, where Lenin's Red Guards seized power in 1917.

SOURCE NOTES

Chapter 1. The Rise of Joseph Stalin

1. Paul Quinn-Judge. "Murder, Inc." *Time*. Time, 29 June 2003. Web. 12 May 2015.

2. Robert C. Tucker. *The Lenin Anthology*. New York: W. W. Norton, 1975. Print. 727–728.

Chapter 2. A Revolutionary in the Making

1. Karl Marx and Friedrich Engels. "Manifesto of the Communist Party." *Australian National University*. Australian National University, 2011. 12 May 2015.

2. Simon Sebag Montefiore. *Young Stalin*. New York: Vintage, 2008. Print. 75.

3. Ibid. 193.

Chapter 3. The Bolshevik Revolution

None.

Chapter 4. Communist Rule

None.

Chapter 5. Stalin's First Five-Year Plan

1. Robert William Davies, Mark Harrison, and S. G. Wheatcroft. *The Economic Transformation of the Soviet Union, 1913–1945*. Cambridge, UK: Cambridge UP, 1994. Print. 151.

2. Dmitri Volkogonov. *Stalin: Triumph and Tragedy*. New York: Grove, 1991. Print. 165.

3. "Hanging Order." *Collectivization and Industrialization*. Library of Congress, 22 July 2010. Web. 12 May 2015.

4. "Gulag." *Encyclopaedia Britannica*. Encyclopaedia Britannica, 2015. Web. 12 May 2015.

Chapter 6. Progress and Suffering

1. "Ukraine." *Encyclopaedia Britannica*. Encyclopaedia Britannica, 2015. Web. 12 May 2015.

2. "Kazakhstan Remembers the Victims of the Holodomor." *Eurasian National University*. Eurasian National University, 31 May 2012. Web. 12 May 2015.

Chapter 7. The Great Terror

1. Vadim Z. Rogovin. *Stalin's Terror of 1937–1938: Political Genocide in the USSR*. Oak Park, MI: Mehring, 1998. Print. 176.

2. "Stalin: Purges and Praises." *BBC*. BBC, 2014. Web. 12 May 2015.

Chapter 8. World War II

1. "Katyn Massacre." *Encyclopaedia Britannica*. Encyclopaedia Britannica, 2015. Web. 12 May 2015.

2. "Operation Barbarossa: The Biggest Military Adventure in History." *Mental Floss*. Mental Floss, 21 June 2011. Web. 12 May 2015.

3. Adolf Hitler. *Hitler's Table Talk, 1941–1944*. New York: Enigma, 2000. Print. 8.

4. "Nazi Persecution of Soviet Prisoners of War." *United States Holocaust Memorial Museum*. United States Holocaust Memorial Museum, 20 June 2014. Web. 12 May 2015.

5. Svetlana Alliluyeva. *Only One Year*. New York: Harper, 1969. Print. 370.

6. Dmitri Volkogonov. *Stalin: Triumph and Tragedy*. New York: Grove, 1991. Print. 427.

SOURCE NOTES CONTINUED

7. Paul Sheehan. "Patriots Ignore Greatest Brutality." *Sydney Morning Herald*. Sydney Morning Herald, 13 Aug. 2007. Web. 12 May 2015.

8. "International: Die, But Do Not Retreat." *Time*. Time, 4 Jan. 1943. Web. 12 May 2015.

9. Max Hastings. *Inferno: The World at War, 1939–1945*. New York: Vintage Books, 2012. Print. XV.

10. J. T. Dykman. "WWII Soviet Experience." *The Eisenhower Institute.* Gettysburg College, n.d. Web. 12 May 2015.

11. Michael Ellman and S. Maksudov. "Soviet Deaths in the Great Patriotic War: A Note." *Europe-Asia Studies* 46.4 (1994): 671–680. Print.

Chapter 9. The Iron Curtain Descends.

1. Winston Churchill. "The Sinews of Peace." *American Rhetoric*. American Rhetoric, 2013. Web. 12 May 2015.

2. Svetlana Alliluyeva. *Twenty Letters to a Friend*. New York: Harper, 1967. Print. 10.

Chapter 10. A Dark Legacy

1. "Joseph Stalin." *American Experience: Race for the Superbomb*. PBS, 2009. Web. 12 May 2015.

2. Svetlana Alliluyeva. *Twenty Letters to a Friend*. New York: Harper & Row, 1967. Print. 142.

INDEX

INDEX CONTINUED

ABOUT THE AUTHOR

Linda Cernak is an independent writer of student texts and teacher educational materials. Her previous experience includes 15 years as an editor and project manager. Since 1994, Cernak has worked as a freelance contributing writer for student and teacher texts in a variety of subject areas and has published numerous classroom readers for social studies, science, and the arts. Her list of published works also includes a series of fiction leveled readers for elementary grade students.